HASTINGS

A Pictorial History

Endpapers: A fine print by C. G. White *c.*1800 entitled
'On the Beach, Hastings' showing two luggers and East Hill
in the background

Frontispiece: 'The renowned Battle of Hastings in Sussex . . .' Hamilton's print showing Harold mortally wounded by an arrow.

HASTINGS

A pictorial history

D. ROBERT ELLERAY, A.L.A.

Fellow of the Royal Society of Arts

PHILLIMORE

1979

Published by
PHILLIMORE & CO. LTD.
London and Chichester
Head Office: Shopwyke Hall,
Chichester, Sussex, England

ISBN 0 85033 324 5

Printed in Great Britain by
UNWIN BROTHERS LIMITED
at The Gresham Press, Old Woking, Surrey

and bound by
THE NEWDIGATE PRESS LIMITED
at Book House, Dorking, Surrey

In Memory of

WINIFRED K. FOX, A.L.A.

and her valuable work for
Local History at Worthing Borough Library

Southward ho! to the cliffs and smoother sands of
ancient and picturesque Hastings!—Hastings is none
of your *parvenu* towns, that can scarce claim an
antiquity of even a couple of centuries; it is a very
ancient and dignified town, with an historical
reputation that no town need feel ashamed of.

The London Journal, 1858

ACKNOWLEDGMENTS

First, my sincere thanks go to John N. Allen, B.A., F.L.A., County Librarian, East Sussex County Library, for generously allowing me to use material from the Local Collections at Hastings and Brighton Libraries. I am also indebted to the following for permission to copy photographs, drawings and other material used in this book: Hastings Museum; J. Manwaring Baines, F.S.A.; Frederick C. Ball; C. R. Edgeley; Philip Savins; the late Henfrey C. P. Smail. In compiling this book I have also used material from my own collection which includes photographs taken by myself and others from the John H. B. Fletcher Collection of Sussex views which is in my possession.

I must also thank the following for their help, advice and comments during my research into the history of Hastings: Miss Elaine Baird, B.A., F.L.A. (Reference Librarian, Brighton Library); Mr. B. G. Purdey, A.L.A. (Area Librarian, Hastings); the Reference Library Staff, Hastings Library; Mr. D. C. Devenish, A.M.A., B.A. (Curator, Hastings Museum).

The photographic work for the book has been carried out by Michael J. Coviello (Worthing), and the MS was typed by Miss Esme Evans, B.A., A.L.A., (Information Librarian, Worthing Library).

CONTENTS

'The renowned Battle of Hastings in Sussex . . .'. Hamilton's print showing Harold mortally wounded by an arrow (*frontispiece*)

Acknowledgments

Introduction

INTRODUCTION

Unlike Eastbourne or Worthing, the modern resort town of Hastings did not develop from a minor village community but grew up in the later 18th century as an extension to one of England's most historic medieval fishing ports. So important is this older dimension of the town's history that some account of it must necessarily preface the description of the modern resort which is the main object of this book.

The origins of the settlement at Hastings appear to have stemmed from the fortuitous combination of the rich Channel fisheries and a reasonably sheltered coastal site with a supply of fresh water where a harbour could be established. By the 8th century or earlier, this favourable spot was being used seasonally by Jutish and other fishermen, and during this period and beyond, the general area surrounding Hastings had become a distinctive sub region isolated to a marked extent by the natural features of forests and the Pevensey and Romney marshes. As a result a large measure of autonomy was exercised by the Hastingas (tribal followers of Haesta), who although subjugated by the Mercian King Offa in 771, remained an identifiable group and eventually gave their name to the main settlement in the area. By 928, Hastings had evidently become a town of some note for it appears in a list of places possessing royal mints and coins struck there in the 11th century are extant. These circumstances had other important results including the effective separation of the area from the South Saxon influence, the development of ties with Normandy, and becoming a leading member of the powerful and influential union of the Cinque Ports. Once this status had been achieved privileges accrued and in particular a strong bargaining position resulted from the town's provision of ships and men towards the protection of England. In the early 11th century, as a consequence of the marriage of King Aethelred II (c.968-1016) to Emma, daughter of Richard the Fearless of Normandy, the Abbey of Fecamp became endowed with lands at Hastings, this circumstance later leading to the choice of the area by William the Conqueror for his invasion of England in the autumn of 1066. Shortly before advancing to attack Harold's army, William set up a temporary fort on top of West Hill above the town, which was later made into a permanent castle by Robert Comte d'Eu whose family retained it until 1248. The grant of land in c.1069 to Robert by William the Conqueror in all probability approximated to the area of the Hastings Rape, and thus included the boundaries of the ancient Hastings Borough which extended from Bulverhythe to Ecclesbourne Glen. In 1090, a collegiate church dedicated to St. Mary was begun within the Castle possibly replacing an earlier Saxon chapel. The Castle, much of which has disappeared owing to sea erosion, was enlarged in the 12th century by Henry II, but following the death of Alice Comtess d'Eu in 1248, both its military importance and condition steadily declined.

For over a thousand years the fortunes of the town of Hastings fluctuated in direct relation to the success or failure of its fishing port, the main threat arising from natural changes in the coast line owing to action by the sea. In 1287 a severe storm wrought great damage to the harbour and it is at this period that the silting up of the port is mentioned as causing a decline in prosperity. A further serious threat developed as a result of the Hundred Years War (1339-1453) between England and France which exposed Hastings to damaging attacks from the sea (in 1339 and 1377), interfered with coastal fishing, and finally, when Normandy was lost, virtually terminated cross Channel trade. In 1500 there were some 30 fishing boats in operation, but by 1587 only 15, and the town's participation in the Cinque Ports' fishing expeditions to the North Sea herring grounds was badly affected. In 1546 reference is made to the town being 'by flux and reflux of the sea and by conflagrations of our enemies . . . reduced to waste, destruction, and poverty'.

Coinciding with the Armada crisis (when the town contributed the ship *Anne Bonaventure*) Hastings received a Charter of Incorporation from Elizabeth I, which confirmed the Borough's many privileges, raised the status of the Bailiff to Mayor, and endowed the town with additional lands, including the 'stone beach' in front of the town. Ten years before Incorporation, the wooden pier or harbour arm which had given some protection to the port was destroyed by a storm, and the structure, subsequently restored in 1595, was yet again washed away in 1597. Since this period right up to the present time the story of Hastings' harbour has been one of frustration—the frequent appeals for its reconstruction whether made in the 16th or 20th centuries, being met with the same indifference. In spite of the harbour difficulties the 17th century witnessed some improvement in the fishing industry, shipbuilding and coastwise trade. In 1641 there was a fleet of 33 vessels, and Hastings was building boats for an area extending from Brighton to the Isle of Thanet, while a coastal traffic in timber, iron, grain and later coal was maintained until the 19th century.

In spite of the importance of the events connected with the Armada and the gaining of a Royal Charter much of the 16th and 17th centuries saw only slight progress in Hastings. In 1700 however, a Town Hall was built replacing the old Court Hall and seven years later John Collier, son of Peter Collier landlord of the *Lamb* Inn Eastbourne, was appointed Town Clerk. This event may be seen as the beginning of a period that witnessed a steady change from the old 'medieval' style town towards a community which began to take advantage of its marine situation to attract visitors and promote growth. Part of the inscription on Collier's monument in St. Clement's Church states: 'He was bred to the

1. A portrait of John Collier, solicitor (1685-1760) who at 25
became Town Clerk of Hastings and later Mayor on five occasions.
Collier's achievements marked a turning point in the town's history,
and his influence, especially with the Pelham family, brought
Hastings many benefits.

practice of the law, by which, with his superior abilities and great application,
he acquired an ample fortune, with a fair character; and at the same time,
eminently displayed his benevolence and hospitality . . .'. Collier died in 1760
having been town clerk for 39 years, and Mayor on five occasions, but the most
significant event in his career was his appointment as agent to the Pelham
family, and so through the influence of the Duke of Newcastle, to become
Surveyor-General of Customs for the County of Kent in 1733. These influential
positions and the consequent high esteem in which he was held by the Pelhams
made it possible for John Collier to obtain financial benefits for Hastings. The
interest of the Pelhams in Hastings was sustained by Edward Milward (1723-
1811) who became Collier's son-in-law in 1754, and succeeded him as the town's
leading citizen, being several times Mayor and also Surveyor-General of Customs.
The Pelham connection also had the important effect of drawing the attention
of nobility to the town, a circumstance which had significant results, when,

towards the end of the century, a number of coastal towns became the object of a new interest deriving from the promotion of the 'sea-water cure', and the benefits of staying by the seaside.

The Rise of the Resort

The modest extent of the old town of Hastings on to which a watering-place was to be grafted in the last quarter of the 18th century may be seen in the map drawn by Samuel Cant in 1746. The plan shows a small cluster of buildings around the Bourne Stream stretching north from the port area to a junction

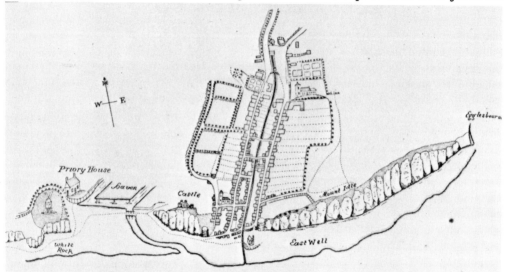

2. Samuel Cant's map of Hastings drawn in 1746.

near All Saints' Church, and little changed since the visit of Daniel Defoe in 1703, when he computed the population as 1500 with some 600 houses. It should be noted that the basic plan of Hastings had evolved rather differently from the usual single main street pattern, the variation resulting in the formation of two streets (High Street and Fisher, later All Saints' Street) of equal importance flanking the central Bourne Stream, linked by a number of small cross lanes and merging at the north end to form an exit route—the Old London Road—out of the valley. By 1600, as a result of the Borough acquiring the 'stone beach' in front of the town, where a defensive wall then existed, a minor extension of the town had taken place called the 'suburb' in what is now the George Street area. Owing to the difficulties presented by the hilly nature of the district, the direction of resort development, when it began in earnest, proceeded south-westwards along the coast. Changes were slow however during the major part of the 18th century, and in 1801, Thomas Pennant[1] wrote 'We descended a long steep hill to Hastings, a town crowded in a narrow gap between high hills, open to the sea; a wild port, without even the shelter of a pier'. Pennant goes on to mention the dominating importance of the town's fishery, a fact confirmed by recent research[2] which reveals that in c.1650, out of the 280 heads of households in the port, 239 were directly concerned with fishing and services connected with the sea.

It was during the year of John Collier's death, 1760, that the first reference to Hastings as a resort appeared in the *Universal Magazine*, giving details of the Regulation Coach journeys between London and the *Swan* Inn in High Street, and commenting 'There are several good families in the place: a card assembly held once a fortnight and a pretty good choice of lodgings, some of which are neat and well furnished'. To reach Hastings by road at this date, however, was both time consuming and hazardous, and this was perhaps a good reason why in 1768 a group of gentlemen failed in their attempt to launch a subscription 'to make Hastings into a bathing place'. Success was not long delayed however, for in 1771 Thomas Hovenden became landlord of the old *Swan* Inn and immediately set about improving its standard of accommodation so as to attract visitors to the town. He announced that hitherto 'the want of better accommodation at the Swan has often been urged as an objection to company coming to Hastings to bathe in the sea' and that in future 'this objection will be removed by the well-known and approved abilities of such a House . . .'. Hovenden's efforts were rewarded—his new Swan Rooms held their first Assembly on 17 August 1772 with great success, and this became a weekly event on Mondays at 6 p.m. From this time there was a steady growth in Hastings of the recognised watering-place amenities, the improvements being stimulated in the early 1790s by a specific recommendation of the town as a place for recuperation and taking the sea-water cure from Dr. Mathew Baillie, F.R.S., Physician Extraordinary to George III. In addition to these favourable circumstances, Hastings, in company with other coastal places in south east England, was also experiencing an increase in prosperity because of the threat of Napoleon's armies—barracks were built at Halton in 1804, troops and their dependents arrived, and the same year saw Sir Arthur Wellesley (later Duke of Wellington) stationed in the town. In 1788 the first circulating library was opened under the direction of John Stell who, six years later, published the town's first Guide. In 1781 Stell's library was purchased by James Barry who set up new premises on East Parade which also provided billiards and a lounge where evening concerts were held. Around 1802 Barry established the resort's first Warm Baths near the library, and by 1814, a 'Bathing Machine Station' was in existence 'to the westward of the town—close to the Marine Parade', the machines being referred to as being 'about thirty very good ones'. A theatre was established in Hastings some time before 1800, but owing to opposition from the local magistrates it was forced to operate outside the Borough boundary and was attached to the *Hare and Hounds* Inn at Ore. Later in 1825 a license was obtained by a Mr. Frederick Brooke to erect a theatre in the Borough, and this was done in Bourne Street—but was only partially successful and closed after seven years existence owing to lack of support.

Once the popularity of Hastings had been established and the number of visitors began to increase, the building of new houses gathered momentum. In 1797 a small Marine Parade was financed by Dr. Samuel Satterley and this was extended by public subscription in 1805. Some years later the Parade was referred to by Parry as being 'a very confined one, though neatly kept, and extremely lively and busily attended; the ship and boat building in the vicinity, accompanied by the multitude of large and hansome pleasure-boats, with occasional small traders, gives it a very cheerful appearance'—a description which suggests a happy

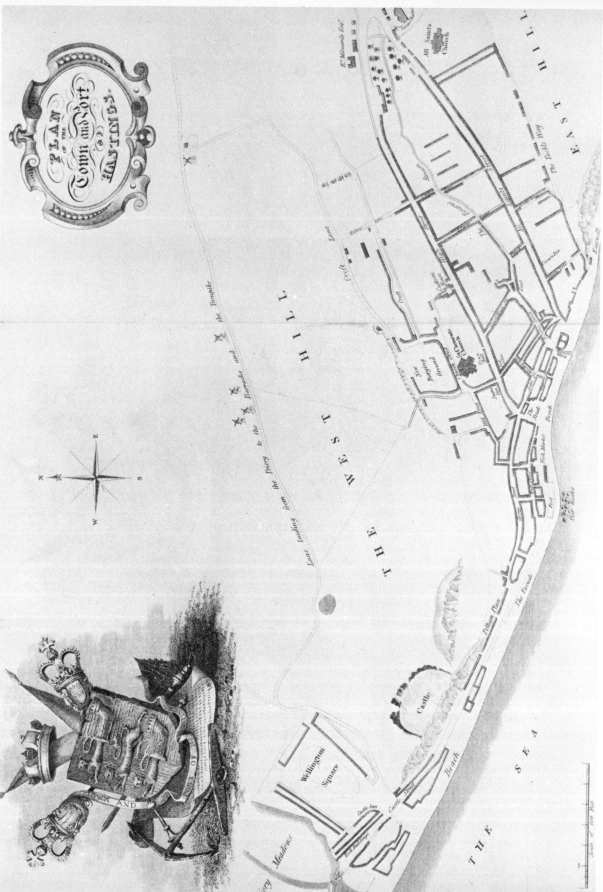

3. W. G. Moss's map published in his *History and Antiquities of Hastings* (1824), showing the first extension of the resort along the coast into the Priory Valley.

co-existence of both resort life and the local fishing industry—a state of affairs which has remained a characteristic feature of the port area. Lodging houses for visitors were erected in 1805 in the Croft but 19 years elapsed before the town's best unit of Regency architecture, Pelham Crescent, was begun in 1824, and in the same year the map published by W. G. Moss shows the progress of the parade development in front of West Hill and thence extending round into Priory Valley. The fashionable Crescent was designed by Joseph Kay, and the whole scheme a speculation planned by Sir Thomas Pelham, 1st Earl of Chichester. It was later flanked by Pelham Place (east) and Breeds Place (west), and its centrepiece, the imposing St. Mary-in-the-Castle, conveniently provided the town's proprietary chapel. The most original feature of the Crescent was the Pelham Arcade, neatly accommodated under the ramped approaches to the chapel, providing baths, a bazaar, and concert room which soon became a popular rendezvous for visitors.

At about the same period that Pelham Crescent was under construction, a further speculation, this time by the local bankers Breeds, Farncomb and Wenham had commenced culminating in the layout of Wellington Square. This was a significant development for it marked the extension of urban growth into the adjacent Priory Valley and the beginning of its transformation into the new Victorian town of Hastings which, by the end of the century, had superseded the old settlement in the Bourne Valley. By the time Wellington Square was completed in the early 1830s, the general economic recession of the period was affecting Hastings in common with many other resorts and growth was considerably curtailed. The next 20 years (1840-1860) however saw an increase in population from 11,789 to 23,443, the main factor in this advance being the arrival of the railway at West Marina in 1845, and in central Hastings in 1851.

By 1830, the westward growth of Hastings had been confronted with an unexpected rival—a large scale speculation by James Burton—the elegant new resort of St. Leonards, described by Doctor A. B. Granville in his *Spas of England* (1841) in the following enthusiastic terms: 'We shall look in vain on any other coast of England for such a range of buildings as those Mr. Burton has raised below St. Leonards Cliff. None but the unrivalled crescents of Bath and Bristol is superior to the Marina of St. Leonards'. James Burton had acquired the land for his venture in 1828 from the trustees of Charles Eversfield for £7,800, and by October 1829 the St. Leonards Hotel (now the Royal Victoria) was opened, and on 30 March 1830 it was announced that the 'new town' was ready to receive visitors, and that 'the shops under the Colonnade facing the sea were also ready for the reception of light genteel trades'. The creation of St. Leonards in such a short space of time involved the deployment of about a thousand labourers, who, with their dependents, produced a period of local prosperity which to some extent modified the depression then afflicting Hastings. The achievement of James Burton at St. Leonards was notable by any standards, but the success of the venture brought off as it was at a time of recession was remarkable, and the choice of the new town for a stay by the Duchess of Kent and the young Princess Victoria in 1834, sealed the fashionable success of Burton's efforts.

The sudden appearance of St. Leonards on the threshold of Hastings complete with Assembly room, chapel, hotels, shops and services, had repercussions—the older town, in the opinion of some, taking on the role of a poor relation. In 1832, the St. Leonards Improvement Act was passed and Commissioners, including James Burton and his sons, appointed. The town, although within the Borough of Hastings, remained an independent authority until 1875, but a feeling of 'difference' between the two places was manifest and towards the end of the century great efforts were made to ensure a feeling of 'equality', but without complete success, as the opinion expressed in Pike's *Views and Reviews of Hastings* (1897), indicates: '[One is] liable to be misled by the separate mention of two names, into the idea that St. Leonards and Hastings form two separate and independent towns, which in fact originally they were. That stage, however, has long since been past, and although St. Leonards retains its distinctive prestige as the specially fashionable quarter, or as it has been called the Belgravia of Hastings, there is no longer any visible, or even imaginary line of demarkation between the two . . .' and this feeling still persists—as J. Manwaring Baines[3] remarks 'Even today . . . some people feel that "St. Leonards", as an address has a *cachet* that "Hastings" somehow lacks'.

The opening of Hastings railway station in February 1851, coincided with important developments at the south end of the Priory Valley where the large plot of waste ground, known as the 'Priory desert' or 'America Ground', had been a problem for the Borough over the years because of the presence of squatters and their huts. In 1850, this Ground was cleared and subsequently developed by Patrick F. Robertson, M.P. for Hastings, whose name was given to two of the new features—Robertson Street and Terrace. The site of the old Priory Bridge over the Priory Stream near the centre of the 'Ground' became the hub of the area and the junction of the main streets of the new Victorian town, this focal point being given the finishing touch a few years later by the addition of the much admired Albert Memorial. In due course important buildings were erected in the vicinity—Teulon's fine church of the Holy Trinity (1858), the Queen's Hotel (1861) and the Gothic style Brassey Institute in 1879. Northward expansion up the Priory Valley progressed steadily along the line of Queen's Road and was in part of a commercial nature, but also included the Cricket Ground, St. Andrews Square and Church (1870), the Gaiety Theatre (1881), and especially, a new Town Hall, the completion of which in 1881 marked the withdrawal of the seat of municipal government from the Old Town. In the following year the area called St. Andrews Garden, opened in 1864, was extended to form the most attractive open space in the town—Alexandra Park. Around the same period much of Victorian Hastings was laid out, including Silverhill, the Blacklands and Milward Estates, and the large development north of the Old Town at Clive Vale, erected by the British Land Company. Meanwhile in the western area rapid growth also took place and during the decade 1870-1880 the development of Warrior Square and the large Eversfield Estate together with Upper Maze Hill brought about the partial amalgamation of Hastings and St. Leonards. In 1881, a scheme backed by C. G. Eversfield, Decimus Burton and Patrick F. Robertson to create a separate township of 'West Hastings' on the still vacant land between Hastings and the Archway was unsuccessful. The eventual linking of Hastings and St. Leonards resulted in the formation of a sea front of impressive dimensions, but including, unlike Eastbourne or

Worthing, a high proportion of shops. Notable also was the variety of architecture along the front, ranging from the neo-classical restraint of St. Leonards, through the typically Victorian central section to the informal mixture of the Old Town in the east—the whole effectively framed by its distinctive physical setting.

During the last quarter of the 19th century Hastings expanded at a rate comparable with other resorts in Sussex and during these years, as indeed for a considerable period before, had been much favoured by writers and artists as a result of the picturesque attractions of the Old Town and some of the best scenic surroundings in Sussex. During these years considerable moves were made to improve the seaside amenities of the town, the most important being the completion in 1874 of the first stage of the White Rocks Baths—a private venture which owing to the lack of adequate capital was never completed. Another failure marked the closing years of the century—the withdrawal of support for the Harbour Scheme.

By 1910, however, when the population had reached 65,556, there were signs of a recession in the town's fortunes leading to a noticeable drop in population to 61,013 in 1911. The causes of this falling off are not easily explicable but the main reasons advanced have been the late development of nearby Bexhill and the keen competition from other large resorts such as Bournemouth and Worthing. The result of this setback for the town's prosperity was the Council's adoption of a policy of major improvements in 1912, the implementation of which during the interwar years formed the first phase of a transition from Victorian to modern Hastings. Following an interruption during 1914-18 large scale plans to reconstruct the promenade were carried out. Operations began with the erection of a bandstand and shelters at the Pier and the demolition of the old East Sussex Hospital opposite, the space being filled by the important new White Rock Pavilion opened by the Prince of Wales (later Edward VIII) in April 1927. The Pavilion especially formed a significant cultural asset, particularly in maintaining and expanding the musical traditions of the town. In 1930 the Corporation took over the old White Rock Baths, reconstructed them at the considerable cost of £100,000, and by 1935, Hastings had rightly become proud of what had been achieved during a 25 year programme of modernisation. Public enthusiasm concerning the 'improvements' was encouraged by the Council—the whole town was said to be 'infected by the virus of progress', and in the *Hastings Guide* for 1935 appeared the slogan 'The 1066 Town with the 1966 Outlook'. From the same Guide (p. 5) the official view of the achievement was stated clearly and confidently: 'The revival of Hastings is an epic story. Those who return to the town after a lapse of years can hardly believe the evidence of their eyes. It stands to the world today as the most remarkable tribute to . . . the virtues of civic enterprise. The Corporation set to work not in haphazard fashion, but according to a definite plan, to develop the town to the utmost . . . over £3m. has been laid out to this end since the [1914-18] War, and private enterprise has ably reinforced the community effort . . .'.

Further moves towards extending and completing these energetic projects to improve the town were prevented by the onset of the second World War, but it is significant that in spite of the very real progress achieved in providing better amenities for the holiday maker, no real growth in the size of the town resulted. The remarkable increase in population which occurred in Worthing—from 22,567 to 69,431, during the period 1900-1950, was matched by stagnation in Hastings— the comparable figures being 65,556 and 65,522. It was not until after the war that this crucial problem of 'standstill' was to be fully considered and a remedial policy worked out.

Hastings since 1939

Hastings, together with Eastbourne, shared the unhappy distinction of being the most bombed Sussex seaside towns during the 1939-45 War, and by the end of the conflict Hastings had suffered 154 fatal casualties and over 15,000 buildings destroyed or damaged by enemy action. Large scale evacuation of residents was begun during the summer of 1940, and during the autumn of the same year air raids had become so heavy and frequent that there were growing demands for anti-aircraft defences to be provided in the town—demands that were met in mid-October, when appropriately, batteries were set up on the 14th—the date of another, older battle, in 1066! Following a comparative lull during 1941 and part of 1942, the next two years were marked by further heavy attacks culmi-nating in the arrival of flying bombs on 15 June 1944, an emergency which led to the installation of additional batteries of heavy AA guns both on the seafront and surrounding hills. It was during this period that one of the most spectacular incidents of the war took place—the direct hit on the old Church of St. Leonard's by a flying bomb coming in from the sea at an altitude of some 25 feet.

The considerable damage to buildings and services in Hastings during the war led to the familiar and difficult period of reconstruction and rehabilitation following the end of hostilities in 1945. The prime objective for Hastings, as for other affected resorts at the time was to restore as speedily as possible the holiday amenities upon which its livelihood depended. Thus priority was given to the repair and rebuilding of hotels as far as the economic stringencies of the time allowed. In common with many other towns during the immediate post war period Hastings was the subject of large scale planning schemes, and in 1945, an 'Outline Development Plan' was put forward for the town by A. Trystan Edwards, F.R.I.B.A.[4] An interesting feature of the scheme was a New Holiday Centre at Bulverhythe, involving a half-mile frontage, and described by Mr. Edwards as 'a more spectacular type of twentieth-century development than any which could take place on the site of demolished buildings on the promenade. If this Centre were created and at the same time the charming and distinguished buildings on the old sea-front were preserved and modernised, Hastings would have the best of both worlds; it would give an example to the whole of England in showing respect for a noble architectrual heritage . . .'. The Bulverhythe development never materialised and the area where it might have taken shape— sometimes referred to as the 'dismal end of the town' remains without substantial change—but possibly even more unfortunate in the long term was that the admirable sentiments of Mr. Trystan Edwards encouraging a sympathetic appreciation of the town's architectural heritage have gone largely unheeded.

By the 1950s it was becoming clear that the relative prosperity of the pre-war holiday industry was not being re-established in a degree adequate to sustain reasonable growth in the town. In addition the lack of suitable employment for young people coupled with a tendency for increased settlement by retired older persons was threatening what was officially termed a 'social imbalance' in the population. The problems connected with these conditions of 'town standstill' understandably became the major pre-occupation of the Borough Council who set about devising a comprehensive development strategy to provide a solution. In 1958 preliminary studies and surveys went forward and negotiations were begun with the London County Council to create a mutually beneficial arrangement by which a substantial number of Londoners might be settled in Hastings with the necessary housing and new industry for employment. Consequently the Hastings Town Development Scheme was published in 1962 (amended in 1965), providing for an eventual settlement of 18,000 people over a period of 18 years with a projected population for the Borough of about 90,000 by 1981. The Scheme was regarded by the Council 'as essential for the prosperity and future well-being of the town', and had the supreme advantage of being almost entirely financed by the L.C.C.

The size of the Scheme with its long-term implications for both the character and environment of Hastings understandably produced considerable reaction and criticism. As a result a Public Enquiry was held early in 1970, the main opposition to the Council's plans coming from the then Battle Rural District Council, whose area would be most affected by any development in the north west corner of the Borough. Concerning the basic environmental implications, the Battle Rural District Council's objection was that not only did the Scheme involve the destruction of delightful countryside, but would also lead inevitably to increased traffic and abnormal pressure for residential growth, the resulting urbanisation itself prompting yet further development. During this period an explanatory campaign entitled 'Expanding Hastings' was mounted by the Borough, including a public meeting in October 1971. In April 1971 the Scheme was approved by the Government with academic modifications—the proposed total was reduced to 15,000, and the proportion of private enterprise houses to be built increased from one third to one half of the total. The decision was probably inevitable, as Mr. Peter Walker Secretary of State for the Environment commented at the time the Scheme would make 'a valuable contribution' to the relief of London's housing problems . . .[5] Following the Local Government changes of 1974, and the resulting proliferation of planning projects, feasibility studies (and even pre-feasibility studies!) the basic principle of the Hastings Scheme was endorsed in the East Sussex County Council's *Structure Plan*. The Scheme in its present form is for development in the Church Wood/Marline Wood areas with additional portions at Filsham, Baldslow and Little Ridge to accommodate 15,000 people up to 1981, with a reserve capacity of 3,000 after that date. The total area involved is 1060 acres, with 'most of the development . . . grouped in the valleys which provide an attractive environment'.

The pre-occupation and excitement generated by the important events since the War in the sphere of planning have perhaps tended to divert attention from the problems of urban renewal and preservation in the older parts of Hastings. The improvements of the interwar period had, with the glaring exception of Marine Court, only minor repercussions on the town's architecture, the main threat up until the 1950s being neglect. Later, however, the considerable damage sustained during the 1939-45 War resulted in numerous insensitive restorations and infillings.

For many preservation in Hastings has meant the Old Town, with perhaps an occasional glance towards St. Leonards—the typically Victorian central area having received little, if any consideration. This circumstance is reflected in the way preservation groups have developed in the town, first the Old Hastings Preservation Society in 1952, then 15 years later Burton's St. Leonards Society, with the appearance of a third to complete the necessary coverage, long overdue. In 1969, Conservation Areas protecting the Old Town and parts of St. Leonards were designated, but as in many instances elsewhere these measures came too late to prevent or modify damage to attractive and historic sections of the town. Particularly unfortunate was the ruthless clearance of the Bourne Street area in the Old Town, and the planting of the large concrete and glass College of Further Education block in Archery Road, St. Leonards in 1962, although thankfully, the completion of the whole projected College site was prevented mainly by the intervention of the Burton's St. Leonards Society. Generally however, the impression given by the treatment and planning of buildings in central Hastings for several years past is one of a widespread underrating of the value of the Victorian town, which by the irony of circumstance actually benefited from the condition of stagnation which allowed much of it to remain undisturbed. In addition two important features of Hastings—the varied and often dramatic changes of a hilly landscape, and the existence of a local stone, diversified and enhanced the work of the Victorian architects and builders—this applying especially to the remarkable number and variety of churches detached villas and terraces frequently occupying distinctive sites and lending much to the general quality of the 'townscape'. These considerations would suggest that the problems of infilling and renewal in Victorian Hastings deserve careful and resourceful resolution.

If, as is to be hoped, the town's ideal of fashioning a vital and more prosperous Hastings is achieved by the end of the century, it would be to the long term benefit of all if the best of Victorian, as well as Regency and Medieval Hastings were improved and retained. It is the present fascinating amalgam of these elements which today makes the town one of the most visually interesting resorts in southern England.

Worthing, December 1978   D. ROBERT ELLERAY

Notes

1. *A Journey from London to the Isle of Wight*, vol. 2, p. 32.
2. G. O. Cowley, 'Sussex market towns 1550-1750'. Unpublished M.A. Thesis, London Univ. 1965.
3. *Burton's St. Leonards*, 1956, p. 45.
4. Described in *Architect and Building News*, 6 April 1945.
5. *Hastings & St. Leonards Observer*, 17 April 1971.

4. The portion of the Bayeux Tapestry showing William leaving Hastings to engage Harold's army. The earliest reference to the Tapestry is in an inventory of Bayeux Cathedral made in 1476. For many years it remained unrecorded in the church but in about 1725 it came to the notice of Dom Bernard de Montfaucon who published drawings of it. After nearly being destroyed in the Revolution, the Tapestry has been on permanent exhibition in the Bishop's Palace near Bayeux Cathedral since 1945.

5. Hastings Castle was built in about 1070 by Robert Count d'Eu, and the collegiate church of St. Mary added some 20 years later. At the end of the 12th century a keep and other buildings were erected by Henry II. Because of sea erosion half the original site has now vanished leaving only the north and east curtain walls together with a reconstructed arch from the church and some other fragments. In 1591, the Castle site was acquired by the Pelham family.

6. A photograph by John H. B. Fletcher of the interior of Hastings Castle in about 1905.

7. The seals of Hastings Corporation. The large 13th-century seal depicts *obverse* a ship with the banners of the Cinque Ports and England; *reverse* St. Michael, Patron Saint of Hastings. The smaller Mayor's seal dates from the 1589 Charter.

8. All Saints', often referred to as the 'upper church', was erected in about 1410 just beyond the area of the medieval town. Like St. Clement's, restoration was directed by Butterfield in the 1870s and the interior retains a mural above the chancel arch depicting Doom. In the graveyard lies 'Old Humphrey' (George Mogridge, 1787–1854), a once popular writer of children's stories and tracts.

9. A print of the pilloried Titus Oates (1649–1705) who was son of Samuel Oates, Rector of All Saints', and for a time a curate at the church. Titus was expelled from Merchant Taylors' School during his first year, and later was imprisoned for perjury concerning outrageous charges made against a Hastings school master whose post he wished to obtain. The climax of Titus Oates's criminal activity was the fabrication of the 'Popish Plot' connected with Charles II and the Jesuits.

10. Moss's view of the entrance to Hastings from the Old London Road in about 1820. This initial glimpse of the town was much admired, and Horsfield makes special reference to the road 'which passes through trees, and is singularly picturesque and beautiful'. All Saints' Church is on the left.

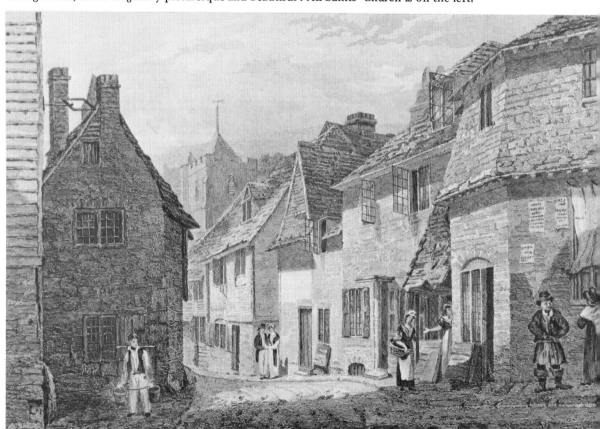

11. The 'View in East Bourn Street', showing the tower of St. Clement's Church, from Moss's *History of Hastings*, 1824.

12. (*above*) Hastings' Perpendicular-style 'Town Church', St. Clement's Croft Road, was rebuilt after the sacking of the town by the French in 1377. In 1875, a full restoration 'in a truly conservative spirit' was completed by William Butterfield. The church has a mayoral pew and several monuments including those of the Milward family and John Collier.

13. A photograph of St. Clement's Church by John H. B. Fletcher taken in about 1898. The Church has a plaque commemorating the marriage of the poet Dante Gabriel Rossetti to Elizabeth Siddall at St. Clement's on 23 May 1860.

14. An engraving of Admiral Sir Clowdisley Shovell (1650–1707), Commander of the Channel Fleet and M.P. for Rochester, 1698–1707. Although born at Cackthorpe, Norfolk, the small timbered house 'Shovells' in All Saints' Street has traditionally been claimed as his birthplace and the residence of the Admiral's mother.

15. (below) The remains of the Town Wall in 1824. This medieval wall extended from the West Fort at the lower end of High Street to the East Fort at the bottom of All Saints Street. The wall, erected c. 1400 was a necessary defensive measure against French raids from the sea and had three gates: Sea Gate (High St.); Water Gate (Bourne St.); and Pulpit Gate (All Saints St.). The wall fell into decay in the mid 18th century and had almost disappeared by 1800.

16. A Town Hall was built in High Street in 1700, paid for by the Borough's M.P.s John Pulteney and Peter Gott, and replaced the old Court Hall. This engraving by Moss shows the Town Hall which was erected on the same site in 1823, and referred to by John Parry in 1833 as 'a mean edifice of inconsiderable size'. The building was vacated in 1881, and since 1949 has housed the town's Local History Museum.

17. Old timbered houses in All Saints' Street in 1909. (*Photograph by John H.B. Fletcher*)

18. Side by side at the north end of High Street stand Old Hastings House (formerly the Mansion), and (right) Torfield House. The Mansion was the home for many years of John Collier and during the 19th century was occupied by Countess Waldegrave, and later, Coventry Patmore. Torfield also dates from the Georgian period, and is possibly a rebuild of a much older structure.

19. (*above*) The Stables Theatre was a conversion in 1958-9, from John Collier's 18th-century stables, which were saved from demolition mainly by the efforts of the Old Hastings Preservation Society. The theatre was opened by Sir Ralph Richardson in June 1959, and in 1975 a £65,000 extension appeal was launched. This photograph by Philip Savins shows the extensions in progress in 1977.

20. The fine vaulted interior of St. Mary Star of the Sea, High Street. The church was designed by Basil Champneys (1842-1935) in 1882-3. The erection of St. Mary's was largely due to the poet Coventry Patmore who contributed £5,000 towards the cost of the church with the intention of making it a memorial to his second wife.

21. The poet Coventry Patmore (1823-1895) succeeded the Countess Waldegrave as occupant of Old Hastings House, High Street, in 1876. Later in 1891, Patmore was forced to vacate the house, a move which caused him 'immense trouble and loss . . . I having built a big Church (St. Mary Star of the Sea) opposite my door, and invested the greater part of my money in local property . . .'

22. (*above*) The chapel of the Convent of Our Lady of Missions, Old London Road was erected in 1924-5 from designs in the Baroque style by John Hicks. The Convent was originally Hastings Lodge (built in 1827) and later the home of Frederick North, Mayor and M.P. for Hastings. From 1884 until 1903, when it became the Convent, the house was the 'Hastings Hydropathic Establishment', using the 'Old Hastings Spring' which rises in the grounds.

23. The Ebenezer Particular Baptist Chapel, Ebenezer Road. At the beginning of the 19th century, a small chapel — the 'Cow Lodge Chapel' was built in Tackleway by the Baptists and was attended by David Fenner. Later, in 1817, the chapel shown here was erected by Mr. Fenner.

4. (*right*) The Swan Inn which stood at the south end of High Street until 1879 was perhaps the most important centre of social and general activity in Hastings for some 400 years. In 1771, Thomas Hovenden became landlord, and the Swan, as the Swan (assembly) rooms played a key role in attracting visitors to the 'new resort' of Hastings.

5. (*below*) An engraved view of Hastings *c.*1780 showing the Stade and the towers of St. Clement's and All Saints' churches.

6. (*right*) Barry's Marine (circulating) library, opened on the Marine Parade in 1791, three years after the resort's first library established by John Stell. Barry's was enlarged in about 1814 by the addition of a first floor billiard room and lounge (as shown here) where musical soirées were held. In 1828 the library was acquired by William Diplock.

27. Another of Moss's views showing the Marine Parade with Parry's Marine Library and bathing machines.

28. Pelham Crescent and St. Mary-in-the-Castle as designed by Joseph Kay in 1824-28, under the auspices of the 1st Earl of Chichester. The construction necessitated the excavation of the cliff face. Unfortunately the demolition of mu{ of Pelham Place (added later on the east side) in 1899 affected the appearance of this fine piece of Regency architectu.

29. (*right*) The Pelham Arcade in about 1825 from a lithograph by C. Hullmandel. The arcade was part of Kay's original design for the Crescent and for many years was a fashionable rendezvous for visitors, providing music, refreshments and a bazaar.

30. Major-General Sir Arthur Wellesley, later Duke of Wellington, was stationed in Hastings, in command of a Brigade during 1806, at the time of the Napoleonic threat of invasion. Much later in 1829, the Duke became Lord Warden of the Cinque Ports.

31. A play-bill dated 17th September 1818
from Hastings' first theatre established at the
Hare and Hounds Inn near Christ Church Ore
sometime before 1800. The theatre was
patronised by several distinguished persons
including Lady Claremont and Earl Somers,
and both Kean (1821) and Elliston acted
there. In 1914, a commemorative plaque
was unveiled on the site by Sir Herbert
Beerbohm Tree (now located at the bottom
of Saxon Road).

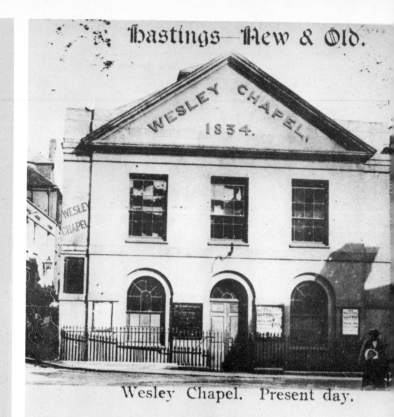

Wesley Chapel. Present day.

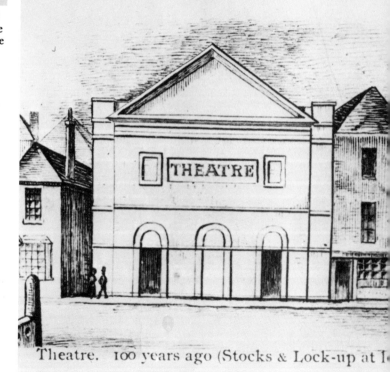

Theatre. 100 years ago (Stocks & Lock-up at l...

32. The old Hastings Theatre, Bourne Street, which was converted into
a chapel by the Weslyans in 1835. The change drew the comment that i...
was a 'disgrace to the town that so fine a building should be sold so che...
for a Methodist Chapel!'. The building survived until 1939, when it was
unfortunately demolished and replaced by the brick Neo-Georgian style
Chapel in use today.

Theatre, Hastings.

On Friday Evening, August 27th,

Will be presented the highly interesting Comedy entitled

EVERY-ONE

HAS

His Fault!

Lord Norland	....	Mr. EDWARDS
Sir Robert Ramble	Mr. CURLING——— Mr. Solus	Mr. GRIFFITH
Mr. Harmony	Mr. FISHER——— Mr. Placid	Mr. SHERARD
Hammond....Mr. LAMBERT	———Porter.....Mr. SPRAY	
Captain Irwin	....	Mr. BARRY
Edward	....	Miss OWEN
Miss Spinster	Miss CRAVEN~———Miss Woburn...	Miss COOKE
Mrs Placid	....	Miss EDWARDS
And Lady Eleanor Irwin......	......	Mrs BROOKE

A Comic Song by Mr. FISHER.

To conclude with (second time, having been received with great applause) the celebrated New and most popular Piece, entitled—THE

BRIGAND

ALESSANDRO MASSARONI, the Italian Robin Hood, was one of those daring spirits that seem to have been created to correct the unequal distribution of good and evil. Chief of a lawless band that infested the mountains near Rome, his name spread terror throughout Italy. No place was secure from his emissaries, and so skilful were his arts of disguise that he was often made the confidant of plots laid by his enemies to entrap him. He made free with the rich, he was liberal to the poor, he was gentlemanly and full of chivalry and romance, and his mode of detention and abstraction, particularly to the ladies, was in such good taste that they admired his gallantry and celebrated his exploits in their songs. A mystery hung over his birth; his mother was a young Florentine, who having been seduced and deserted, died of a broken heart. His exploits are most ably dramatized in this admirable piece.

Alessandro Massaroni, the Brigand Chief......................		Mr. CURLING
Albert......⎱ Students of the French Academy,	⎰Mr. SHERARD	
Theodore....⎰	⎱Miss EDWARDS	
Nicolo, Steward of the Cottage of St. Arnulph		Mr. GRIFFITH
Cardinal Secretary ....Mr. SPRAY———Count Caraffa............		Mr. LEFFLER
Fabio ....Mr. FISHER———Rubaldi, Lieutenant of the Brigands....Mr. EDWARDS		
Spoletti....⎱ Brigands,	⎰Mr. SPRAY	
Carlotti....⎰	⎱Mr. LAMBERT	
Prince Bianchi, Governor of Rome...........................		Mr. BARRY
Ottavia, the Governor's Niece........Miss OWEN		
Maria Graze, Massaroni's Wife....................Miss COOKE		

LOWER BOXES 3s.—UPPER BOXES 2s. 6d.—PIT 1s. 6d.—GALLERY 9d.

Second Price:—LOWER BOXES 2s.—UPPER BOXES 1s. 6d.—PIT 1s.—GALLERY 6d.

Second Price at Half-past Eight.---Children Half-Price.

☞Days of Playing, Mondays, Wednesdays, and Fridays.

33. Another playbill, possibly from the Bourne Street Theatre which opened on 18 August 1825. Although initially popular and presenting such actors as Charles Kemble (1831), the Theatre only survived eight years before convertion into a chapel.

34. Pelham Place in about 1860 showing the 'Russian Gun' on the right. In 1898-9 nearly the whole of Pelham Place was demolished to make way for the Marine Palace of Varieties.

35. Wellington Square in about 1830. The Square, once the site of lime kilns, was developed by the bankers Breeds, Farncomb & Wenham c.1820 as Wellington Place (now the east side). On the left is the Castle Hotel, the recent demolition of which did much to spoil the atmosphere of the Square.

36. (*above*) A wonderfully atmospheric and evocative lithograph of Hastings and East Hill in about 1800, by G. Rowe.

37. The grand entry of the Duchess of Kent and her daughter Princess (later Queen) Victoria, into Hastings on 4 November 1834. As the visitors were greeted by the Mayor, William Scrivens, a Royal Salute was fired from East Hill, and the procession then moved on to St. Leonards. The house behind the triumphal arch is Hastings Lodge, now the Convent of Our Lady of Missions, Old London Road.

38. (*overleaf*) 'The Russian Gun' — a 32 pounder, described as a 'Crimean Trophy', was exhibited for many years on the sea-front opposite Pelham Place. It was eventually removed to the Museum grounds at John's Place and taken for scrap during the 1939-45 War.

39.   A fine print by C. G. White *c.*1800 entitled 'On the beach, Hastings' showing two luggers and East Hill in the background.

40.   W. G. Moss's view of the Hastings fishing fleet and net shops from East Well (entrance to East Hill lift) in *c.*1822.

41. (*right*) Heavy seas invading the promenade opposite Pelham Crescent in the great storm of Sunday, 14 November 1875.

42. The old Rotunda Fish Market which used to stand near the south end of High Street. Built in 1870 it provided for the retail sale of fish.

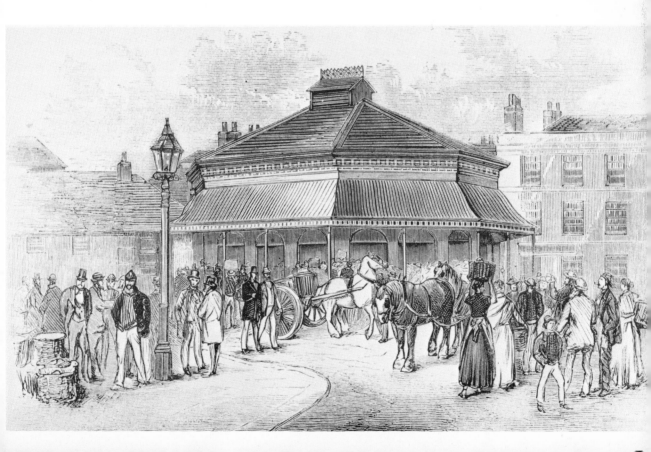

43. (*above*) A photograph by John H. B. Fletcher of the Stade in 1909 with a typical Hastings lugger.

44. (*right*) The East Hill Lift was designed by P. H. Palmer, Borough Engineer, in 1901-3, and has the steepest gradient of any like system in the country. The power until 1974 was supplied by a water balance device, each car having a 600 gallon tank. In 1891 the West Hill Lift was opened by a private company, and later taken over by the Council in 1947. This lift operates through a 462 foot tunnel between George Street and Castle Hill.

45. (*below*) The famous Hastings net shops or 'deezes' unique, photographed by John H. B. Fletcher in 1909. The style of these structures is possibly early 17th-century, and their tall form reflects attempts to utilise limited space and facilitate the storage of nets.

46. (*right*) The Fishermen's Society and Institute in All Saints' Street. The Society was founded by Sophia Mendam, and established in the present building (formerly Hughenden Hall) in 1882. It is also the Headquarters of the famous Winkle Club.

47. The old Lifeboat House which stood in East Parade until about 1950. It was erected on the site of the Custom House in 1882. The first Lifeboat station was established in 1858, when the boat *Victoria* (1858-63) was launched. The present Lifeboat *Fairlight* came into service in 1964.

48. The former Marine Palace of Varieties, or Hippodrome, was designed by Ernest Runtz in 1897-99 and its opening programme included Marie Lloyd and the Tiller dancers. Later the Palace became the Royal Cinema de Luxe, and amusement centre. In 1970 the building was converted into a Bingo Club and amusement centre and much of the attractive neo-baroque interior altered.

49. The south end of All Saints' Street showing (left) the Tudor style 'Pulpit Gate' commemorating one of the gates in the wall which once protected the sea end of the town from attack. On the right is the sadly neglected East Cliff House, built by the Shakespearian critic Edward Capel in 1762, and which has become a prominent eyesore on the seafront since the war.

50. The old Hastings fishing fleet providing a timeless background for figures on the promenade in around 1897.

51. (*right*) A sea angling festival near East Cliff in about 1909. The new East Hill Lift can be seen on the right, and below the Stade with fishing boats.

52. (*below*) A sketch of the projected Harbour planned in 1889 by Mr. Carey. The scheme was at first enthusiastically backed by the town, and provided railway port facilities via a tunnel through East Cliff. In 1890 a Hastings Harbour Act was passed, but difficulties over capital delayed and finally halted the construction.

53. (*below*) The Stade from the south end of Tackleway showing the ruinous condition of the harbour arm. Despite the historic importance of the Old Town's fishing area the arm has been left with only minimal repairs for nearly 80 years. In 1950 the cost of restoration was calculated at £334,000, and today estimates run to three million! Recently a scheme has been suggested by the local Chamber of Commerce costing £48,000, using concrete caissons.

(*above*) Preliminary work on the new Harbour
~~eme~~ in 1896. As the construction advanced serious
~~blems~~ were set by the irregular nature of the sea
~~d~~ and the situation was further aggravated by short-
~~of~~ funds. After the completion of part of the wes-
~~n~~ arm work ceased when the Corporation refused
~~guarantee~~ a sum of £3000 a year to allow the har-
~~ur~~ to be finished.

. St. Nicholas, the Fishermen's Church, East
~~iff~~ was built by the Rector of St. Clements' in
~~54~~, and remained in use until the 1939-45 War,
~~en~~ it was used as a military store and suffered
~~nsiderable~~ damage. In 1955-6 the building was
~~stored~~ and converted into a fishermen's museum
~~th~~ the last of the old Hastings luggers — *Enterprize*
the main exhibit.

56. (*opposite*) George Street, with its informal architecture and extraordinary variety of shops, can claim to be the most attractive and lively thoroughfare in Hastings. This photograph looking eastwards dates from about 1894.

57. A similar view of George Street in 1978, showing remarkably little change in the appearance of the buildings since the late 19th century.

58. In 1844 the small steamer *Waterman* belonging to the Waterman Steam Packet Company struck the dangerous Castle rocks off Hastings and nearly sank. Later the damage was repaired and she was refloated.

59. The White Rock headland which formerly stood just west of Priory Valley. The Rock became more and more of an obstacle to development along the coast in the early 19th century and was removed in 1834-5.

60. The old Infirmary and Verulam Place in about 1850. The town's first Infirmary was opened in 1834 in the old
Royal Oak building in High Street.

61. The old Infirmary on the sea front at White Rock was erected in 1841 and enlarged two years later. In 1887 the
building was replaced by the red brick East Sussex Infirmary, shown here, which in turn was demolished in 1912-13,
the site being later used for the White Rock Pavilion opened in 1927.

62.   The White Rock Pavilion was opened during the visit of the Prince of Wales (later Edward VIII) in April 1927, and provided the town with a much needed concert hall. The attractive Spanish Colonial design was by C. Cowles-Voysey and H. S. Morgan. Over the years many famous orchestras and musicians have performed in the Pavilion.

63.   A print from the *Illustrated London News* of the Queen's Hotel, which opened in December 1862. The design was by F. H. Fowler in a modest Italianate style, although much of the detail, including the towers, has now gone. Contemporary comment was that the hotel would be 'a most valuable acquisition . . . and well appreciated by aristocratic visitors'.

64. Musicians and bystanders on the front — a photograph dating from about 1880.

65. (*overleaf*) Hastings Regattas have been held since around 1820, and in the last quarter of the 19th century events were enlivened by keen rivalry between crews from Hastings and St. Leonards. The print reproduced here shows a regatta off the Old Town in about 1885.

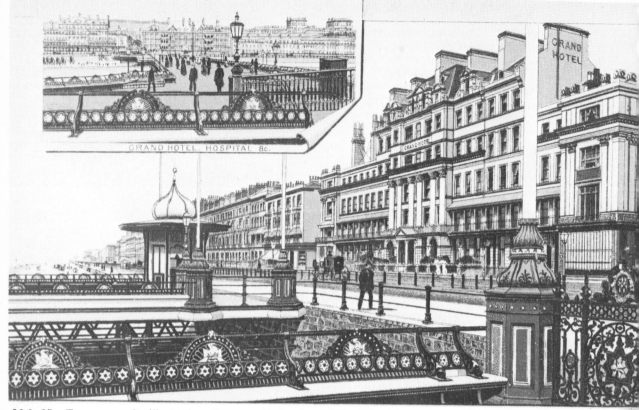

66 & 67. Two composite illustrations from a guide book *c.*1890 of Hastings seafront. The top view shows the once popular Grand Hotel (the site is now vacant), and provides some nice detail of the Pier's cast iron work.

68. Enjoying the winter season at Hastings — Victorian style. A sketch from the *Daily Graphic*, November 1890.

69. Palace Chambers, White Rock was erected as the Palace Hotel in 1886, and designed in a flamboyant classical free style by Arthur Wells.

70. Holiday crowds on Hastings beach in about 1898. Note the carefully regimented bathing machines.

71. Late Victorian seafront scene with sailing boats at Denmark Place.

72. Late Victorian beach scene with pleasure boats.

73. (*right*) A view of Hastings Pier from a folding guide *c.* 1890. In about 1912 the shore end kiosks were removed prior to a complete remodelling of the entrance area. Subsequently additional buildings have completely altered the original proportions of the promenade deck.

74. (*above*) Hastings Pier in about 1903. The design was by Eugenius Birch and the construction carried out by R. Laidlaw of Glasgow in 1869-72, at a cost of £23,000. The south pavilion was destroyed by fire in July 1917, and rebuilt in its present form.

75. (*right*) Passing the time of day at Hastings Pier — an illustration from *The Pictorial World* dated September 1875.

76. (*overleaf*) Hastings beach in about 1895 showing one of the vanished delights of the English seaside — the itinerant pierrot show with attentive audience.

THE
HASTINGS
POLKA

INTERIOR OF PAVILION ON THE PIER HASTINGS.

BY
C.H.R. MARRIOTT.

Ent. Sta. Hall.

PRICE 3
DUET 4
Full Orchestra 2 nett
Septett 4

Published by
J. DORMAN,
22. GRAND PARADE. ST LEONARDS

77. An attractively illustrated music cover showing the interior of the Hastings Pier Pavilion Concert Hall in about 1890 (burned down in 1917). C. H. R. Merriott, composer of the 'Hastings Polka', was a well known local violinist and for several years conducted the pier orchestra.

. On 15 April 1919 the German U-Boat UII8 was stranded on Hastings beach near Harold Place. The submarine had broken tow in rough seas while being taken from Harwich to Cherbourg for use by the French Navy. She was later broken in situ after schemes for placing her on permanent display in Warrior Square had been rejected.

9. The beached German U-Boat, from a postcard published at the time.

80. (*above*) A view of the mouth of the Priory Valley in 1850 showing the America Ground shortly before the development of the Robertson Street and adjacent areas.

81. (*left*) Patrick F. Robertson, the London merchant who gave his name to Robertson Street and Terrace. Robertson first contested Hastings as a Conservative candidate unsuccessfully in 1847, but was elected M.P. at a second attempt in 1852, and on a number of subsequent occasions until 1869. In 1849 he leased part of the 'America Ground' for 99 years and developed it.

82. Looking down Robertson Street towards the Albert Memorial in about 1875.

THE ALBERT MEMORIAL FROM ROBERTSON S!

83. Hastings Railway Station soon after its opening in 1851, from a lithograph by Graf. The beginning of the town's railway history was marked by acrimonious disputes between the South Eastern Railway Company and the L.B.S.C.R. concerning the joint use of the section between Bopeep Junction and Hastings. Eventually agreement was reached in 1854.

84. Sarah, Countess Waldegrave was a notable benefactor to charitable causes in mid 19th-century Hastings. She was the daughter of the joint Rector of All Saints' and St. Clement's, William Whitear, and first married the younger Edward Milward (died 1833), and then the Eighth Earl Waldegrave. She died in 1873, 11 years after the erection of the fountain in Robertson Street by public subscription 'In grateful recognition of the constant support affected by her to the religious and benevolent institutions of the Borough'.

85. Holy Trinity, Robertson Street was designed by Samuel Saunders Teulon, and completed in 1858. The church is a fine example of Gothic Revival architecture ingeniously fitted into a difficult site, and the dedication commemorates the old Priory of the Holy Trinity founded nearby in the 12th century by Sir Walter Bricet.

86. (*right*) A composite illustration from the *Illustrated London News* showing scenes at the opening of the Town Hall by the Mayor, W. F. Revill, in September 1881.

87. (*left*) J. G. Shorter's drawing which appeared in the *Illustrated London News* of the magnificent banquet which was put on by the Borough for the visit of the Lord Mayor of London in 1850.

88. (*below*) The Mayor and Mayoress of Hastings in holiday mood! — opening the Battle of Confetti on the sea-front during the Hastings and St. Leonards Carnival in 1895.

89. (*left*) Thomas Brassey (1838-1918; knighted 1881, Baron 1886, 1st Lord Brassey 1911) was Mayor and also Liberal M.P. for Hastings from 1868 to 1885, and a notable benefactor to the town. His distinguished public career was particularly concerned with naval affairs, and he was Civil Lord to the Admiralty 1880-84. He founded the yearbook *Brassey's Annual*, and wrote a major work on British naval history (1882-83).

90. (*right*) The Brassey Institute was presented to the town in 1879 by Thomas Brassey 'to provide for intellectual and artistic development among the inhabitants'. The Venetian Gothic design was by a local architect, W. L. Vernon. The Institute comprised a museum, class rooms and a library and today still houses the town's Public Library. The Museum was transferred to John's Place in 1928.

91. (*far right*) The second Lady Brassey. Three years after the death of his first wife (Anna Allnut), Lord Brassey married Sybil de Vere Capell, daughter of Viscount Malden in 1890.

92. (*left*) The built at Catsfie dence. Followi accident in 191 became St. Hila military occupa

93. (*right*) The and his first wi later described *the Sunbeam* (with 350 HP m as an auxillary and broken up

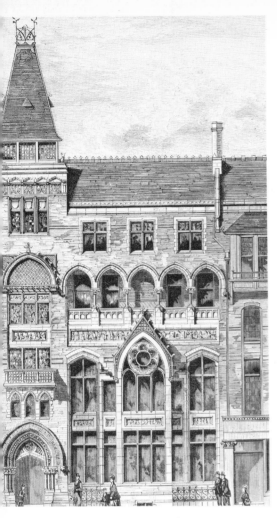

...eau-style Mansion Normanhurst was
...as Brassey in 1865-71 as a family resi-
...c death of the 2nd Earl Brassey in a road
...manhurst Estate was sold, and the Mansion
...chool in 1922. After extensive damage by
...39-45, it was demolished in 1951.

...ht *Sunbeam* in which Thomas Brassey
...de a round-the-world trip in 1876-7,
...assey's best selling book *The Voyage of
...beam* was a topsail schooner (351 tons)
...ned by St. Clare J. Byrne. After serving
... she was sold to the Runciman family

94. (*above*) A recent photograph of the Town Hall showing the north elevation with the elaborate Council Chamber window (left) and cross gabled roof. The Town Hall now provides a gallery for the permanent display of the Hastings Embroidery.

95. (*below*) In 1805 the Independents (Congregationalists) acquired a site in the Croft and erected a wooden chapel which had been specially pre-fabricated in London and shipped to Hastings. This chapel, shown here, was replaced by a brick church in 1877, which survived until 1972.

96. 'Charles New of Hastings' was the driving force behind the expansion of Congregationalism in the town during the years 1869-1912. A Cornishman, New trained at Cheshunt Theological College, and as pastor consolidated the work begun at Robertson Street by James Griffin in 1858. The great achievement of New's career was the opening of the new Robertson Street Church in 1886 at a cost of £12,000.

97.   The old Central Methodist Church occupies a key site in Cambridge Road and since 1875 has given that road much of its character. Disused since 1974, and now sadly under threat of demolition, the church was designed by W.W. Pollock at a cost of £8,000, the foundation stone being laid by Lady Brassey.

98.   Chess Champions 1895. The first Hastings Chess Tournament was held at the Brassey Institute in August 1895, and organised by Councillor H. E. Dobell. Twenty-two competitors took part from Britain, the United States, Germany, France, Italy, Austria, Canada and Russia. This cartoon drawing shows the first Champion Harry N. Pillsbury (top right, U.S.A.) who received a prize of £150. In 1904 Hastings was chosen by the newly formed British Chess Federation as the venue for its first conference.

99.   (right) The Gaiety Theatre Queens Road was designed by Cross & Wells and opened as a private venture by George Gaze on 1 August 1882. Gaze remained in charge until his death in 1904, and after many years of varied productions including repertory, musical comedy, pantomime and opera, the Gaiety was converted into a cinema in 1933.

100.   (left) In March 1891, Mr. Gladstone visited Hastings at the invitation of the Home Counties Division of the National Liberal Federation. After being greeted by Lord Brassey and an enthusiastic crowd of many thousands at Warrior Square Station, Gladstone addressed a meeting at the Gaiety Theatre, as shown here in a drawing from the Daily Sketch.

101. (*above*) The St. Clement's Caves in the Ashdown sandstone of West Hill have been a tourist attraction for some 150 years. The owner of the land, Edward Milward sealed the entrance in about 1810 but later a visitor broke into the caves, and in 1827, a local trader, Joseph Golding, obtained permission to open them to the public. The caves served as air raid shelters during the 1939-45 War.

102. An illustrated advertisement for St. Clement's Caves published *c.*1890.

103. (*left*) Mr. D. Furroll, Poulterer and Fishmonger displaying his Christmas stock at 50, Queen's Road in about 1895.

104. Messrs. Lewis, Hyland & Co., general outfitters opened in Queen's Road in 1888. The shop was a branch of the business originally established by Mr. Lewis at Ashford Kent, in 1820.

105. Mr. Dick Russell, Riding and Job Master. Mr. Russell ran a successful Livery Stables at St. Andrews Mews, Queen's Road in the 1890s, and later moved into the motor coach business.

106. One of Mr. Russell's Motor Coaches about to start on a sightseeing tour in about 1912.

107. Late Victorian Hastings — the
Memorial and surrounding streets in
about 1896.

108. The Albert Memorial Clock Tower until recently formed a pleasant focus at the intersection of the town's main shopping streets. The Tower was erected in 1862 from a winning design by the Liverpool architect E. A. Heffer which included a statue of the Prince Consort by Edwin Stirling. In 1973 fire badly damaged the top of the Memorial including the clock and unfortunately this characteristic piece of Victorian Hastings was demolished.

109. The centre of Hastings in 1978 — Now bereft of much of its identity since the demolition of the Memorial.

110. A balloon ascent from the Cricket Ground, possibly connected
with one of the election campaigns conducted between 1906 and 1910.

111. (*above*) St. Andrew's Square, a late Victorian
development on a modest scale, has for many years
been the site of the Salvation Army Barracks. Long
known as the 'Iron Fort', the buildings were substan-
tially enlarged in 1937.

112. The Unitarian Free Christian Church, South
Terrace provides a very late example of the neo-
classical style in 19th-century church design. The
Unitarians after holding temporary meetings in the
Music Hall and Swan Inn from 1860, opened the permanent church shown here in May 1868. The foundation
stone was laid by Sir John Bowring.

113. Robert Tressell (i.e. Robert Noonan) 1870-1911, was a talented sign writer and decorator of Irish extraction who worked in Hastings during the first decade of this century. In the remarkable novel *The Ragged Trousered Philanthropists*, Tressell revealed himself as the Socialist chronicler of 'the other Hastings', or 'Mugsborough', as he called the town. Tressell's biographer F. C. Ball writes 'On paper Noonan's character may appear over-serious, but in life it was compensated by a droll fund of humour and his enthusiastic nature'.

114. An eye-catching example of Robert Tressell's craftsmanship executed on the wall of a local house in around 1907. Tressell was for a time employed by Adams and Jarrett, and can just be seen at the end of the word 'Branches' below the advertisement.

15. The chancel of St. Andrew's Church, Queens Road,
showing the mural decoration executed by Robert Tressell
in 1905. It is ironic that the centenary of Tressell's birth
was marked in Hastings by the destruction of this church.
In 1966 the chancel walls were daubed by vandals and
overpainted, but much of the design was rescued in fragments by Mr. Frederick C. Ball and others during demolition in 1970.

16. (right) The former St. Andrew's Church, Queen's
Road demolished in 1970. The church was designed by
Habershon & Brock in 1869, and the site together with
£1,000 was given by the Misses Sayer of Hastings.

117. The old Hastings Gas Offices in Queens Road provide a good example of Victorian cream and red brickwork. Above the central porch is the date 1878, and the tall central tower may well have been designed in deference to the adjacent St. Andrew's Church (1869), destroyed in 1970.

118. Alexandra Park in about 1905. This large Park is one of the most attractive features of Hastings, and the lower section known as St. Andrews Gardens was established as a subscription garden in 1864. Later in 1882, it was enlarged and opened as Alexandra Park by the Prince and Princess of Wales. The Park has considerable botanical interest and its lakes and ponds are fed by the Old Roar stream.

119.   A cricket match at the Central Ground near the Town Hall. There is a long and vigorous tradition of cricket in Hastings — the Hastings Cricket Club was founded in 1840, and in 1872 the Central Ground was opened on land once part of the old Priory Farm and purchased from the Cornwallis Estate for £5,000. The ground has been the venue for the Hastings Cricket Week since 1887.

120.   Hastings Cricket Ground showing the pavilions and part of South Terrace and (left) Devonshire Road. The Ground, in addition to its importance for sport, considerably enhances the environment of central Hastings by providing a pleasant open space in a congested area, yet in recent years, and especially in 1978, moves have been made to develop the area!

121. (*overleaf*) Hastings Railway Station in the age of steam *c.*1910. Much of the station was rebuilt in 1931, and the coastal services were electrified and began operation on 7 July 1935.

122. (*left*) One of the sights of Hastings — especially for the industrial archaeologist — is the magnificent iron railway bridge at the north end of Queens Road with massive fluted columns. The bridge dates from 1898 and replaced the brick St. Andrew's Tunnel.

123. (*below*) Looking towards West Hill from the south end of Alexandra Park with the fine mid-Victorian villa 'Saxonhurst' on the right. Beyond the massive iron railway bridge can be seen the typical Hastings townscape of tiered houses and terraces.

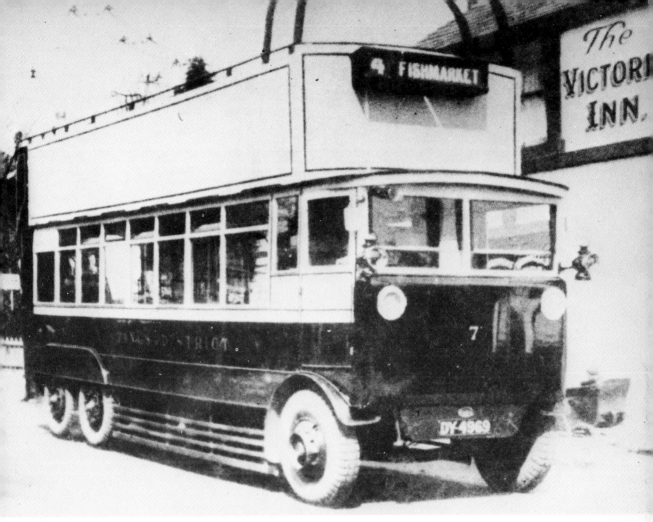

124.   One of the original fleet of Hastings' trolleybuses — an open top Guy BTX with a Dodson body. Trolleybuses were introduced in place of trams in 1928, and after being taken over by the Maidstone & District Company in 1957, were withdrawn on 31 May 1959. In 1953 one of the old BTX vehicles — 'Happy Harold', was restored and took part in the Coronation celebrations.

125. (*left*) The Twitten at the top of St. James's Road, Twittens, passages and connecting flights of steps form a characteristic element in the Hastings townscape.

126. Emmanuel Church, West Hill, which occupies a prominent place in Hastings' townscape. The 13th-century style church was erected in 1873-4 and designed by the local architects A. W. Jeffery & Skiller. It narrowly missed destruction in May 1942, when the adjacent Vicarage was bombed causing the tragic death of the incumbent's (Rev. J. Battersby) infant daughter.

127. Summerfields (Bohemia House, just north of the Museum) in about 1910. The destruction of this fine Regency mansion by the Borough in 1972 was an architectural loss to the town. The house was a rebuild in 1817 of Bohemia Farm, which stood on the site of the ancient Crotesley Manor, one of Lord Godwin's possessions. The house was occupied by Princess Matilda of Gloucester during the summer of 1830, and later became a school.

128. The present Hastings Museum at John's Place, Cambridge Road. The Tudor-style building was erected in about 1925 as a private house and later the collections were transferred there from the Brassey Institute in 1928. In 1931-2 an extension (left) was built to provide an art gallery and accommodation for the Brassey Collection (acquired during the voyages of the *Sunbeam*) which became the Durbar Hall.

129. (*opposite page*) The Fire Brigade's spectacular Arch of Welcome to the Prince of Wales in April 1927 — the view shows the Memorial (demolished 1974) from the south end of Queen's Road.

130. (*above*) The Prince of Wales, later Edward VIII, laying a wreath at the War Memorial in Alexandra Park in April 1927.

131. A Commemorative gathering at Hastings Castle in May 1966, to mark the 900th Anniversary of the Battle of Hastings. Other events held during the Anniversary were an Ox Roast at St. Clement's Caves (May 26); presentation of the Freedom of Hastings to Sir Robert Menzies (July 21), and a special service at Battle Church led by the Archbishop of Canterbury (May 16).

132. St. Leonards Pier (latterly also known as the 'Palace Pier') was opened by Lord and Lady Brassey in October 1891, and survived until 1951. The Pier was designed by R. St. George Moore, and built by Head Wrightson at a cost of £30,000. The most elegant feature of the Pier was the pavilion running parallel with the promenade some 200 feet from the shore approached by a special carriage way. Later a second pavilion was completed at the sea end and further alterations were carried out in 1909. The pier was severely damaged in the 1939-45 War.

133. John Foulon's synoptic view of Burton's new town in 1834, indicating the formal marine facade backed by a delightful silvan area (Subscription Gardens, Archery Ground, Maze Hill) where a more relaxed planning, often with Gothic designs, took place over the years.

134. (*right*) James Burton (1761-1837) an influential Scottish architect and builder, founded the new town of St. Leonards in 1828. Burton worked with John Nash on several important London developments including Regents Street and Regents Park, and was also responsible for much of Bloomsbury, and an estate at Tunbridge Wells.

135. Burton's St. Leonards (later Royal Victoria) Hotel was the centrepiece of his seafront design, but in 1904 the building was largely spoilt by 'improvements'. In front can be seen the elegant Baths (now demolished), while on the left, part of the Public Rooms, later the Masonic Hall.

136. A closer view of the original St. Leonards Hotel, Public Rooms (behind the Hotel) and Seafront Baths.

'The renowned Battle of Hastings in Sussex . . .' Hamilton's print showing Harold mortally wounded by an arrow.

37. Louis Philippe was proclaimed 'King of the French, by the grace of God and the will of the people' in the revolution of 1830. In 1848 Louis was deposed, and the following year he and his wife Amelie, as the 'Count and Countess of Neuilly' stayed for a time at the Royal Victoria Hotel, St. Leonards.

38. Charles Haywood Southall's Royal Victoria Library opened to the public in 1831, and occupied the east end of the baths building in front of the St. Leonards Hotel. The circulating library also served as a post office, bank, and housed a printing press.

Drawn by I.Pouton.

Printed by C.Hullmandel.

Published by C.H.Southall, Librarian, Book & Printseller.

139. A race meeting at Filsham Valley, Bopeep, St. Leonards, in September 1826. The event was a great success and is said to have attracted a crowd of 6000. Meetings continued at Bopeep for some years. In the background can be seen one of the Bulverhythe Martello Towers.

140. John Foulon's drawing showing St. Leonard's Church and part of the Marina including Victoria House (now Crown House) in 1834. The church was opened as a proprietary chapel in 1832 and its size did not please John Parry who wrote 'It is to be regretted that the style and proportions are not on a grander . . . scale — it cannot be fairly said to be worthy of St. Leonards . . .'

141. (*above*) The interior of the old St. Leonard's Church. Only five years after completion, in 1837, a section of the cliff behind the building collapsed destroying the chancel which was later replaced on a smaller scale. St. Leonard's was the only church designed by James Burton, and the foundation stone was laid on 8 September 1831 — the Coronation of William IV and Queen Adelaide.

142. (*right*) The new St. Leonard's Church was opened in 1961, and designed by Sir Giles and Adrian Gilbert Scott in a contemporary style with paraboloid arches. The existence of the old church (on the same site) was violently terminated by a flying bomb on 29 July 1944.

143. The St. Leonards Archway (originally East Lodge) which until 1895 marked the seafront boundary between Hastings and the 'new town'. Feelings ran high over the proposed demolition of the Arch, which was said to have 'Lost its significance except as a monument of obsolete aristocratic exclusiveness'. The Council however, took the precaution of demolishing the Arch by night so as to avoid trouble from militant conservationists!

144. The South Colonnade about six years before its demolition in 1929. The Colonnade was completed in 1828 as a unit of shops standing in front of the Marina facade (just south east of Marine Court). As this photograph shows, the once elegant building had degenerated considerably by the end of the 19th century.

145. Marine Court overshadowing Burton's elegant seafront facade. The Court, aptly described by Pevsner as 'the first modernistic affront to the English seaside', completely destroys the scale of surrounding buildings over a wide area. Often referred to as the 'Queen Mary', Marine Court was erected in 1937-38 from designs by Dalgleish & Pullen.

146. A lithograph of the Subscription Garden c.1845 which occupies a small valley north of the St. Leonards Assembly Rooms. On the left is the Clock House — 'a pretty Gothic building' originally designed as a clock tower but later enlarged into a dwelling. Like many buildings in St. Leonards the Clock House was nearly lost by neglect, but has been recently restored.

147. The delightful Gothic Clock House Maze Hill was erected in 1830 when the Pleasure Gardens, now St. Leonards Gardens, were laid out. In 1974 it was estimated that about £10,000 was needed to restore the building and due to the efforts of Mrs. Marie Lebrock and others the repairs were completed in 1976.

148. The Tudor-style North Lodge Maze Hill was erected in 1830 at the northern extremity of Burton's St. Leonards with the new northbound road passing beneath its archway. Shortly after the First World War the author Sir Rider Haggard purchased the Lodge and lived there for several years.

149. *(right)* The fine group of buildings by Decimus Burton in Quarry Hill formerly the Uplands School for Girls, and now part of the College of Further Education. Beyond is the contrasting Tudor-style 'Hazelton', a major design by Norman Shaw erected in 1877-79.

150. Planning disasters apparently never come singly! Until the 1960s one supposed that nothing comparable to Marine Court could again be inflicted on St. Leonards — but it has — this time in the secluded and beautiful area of the Archery Grounds (Archery Road).

151. Warrior Square in about 1900. The Square, developed during 1853-1864, was claimed to be 'the largest and finest in England' comprising 'many majestic mansions . . . undoubtedly some of the best in the borough'. In fact opinions differ sharply concerning the Square, Clunn (c.1923) describing it as 'of noble appearance'; while Pevsner (1962) remarks that it is 'as architecture — nil'.

152. The Royal Concert Hall was erected on the south side of Warrior Gardens in 1878-9 at a cost of £15,000. The hall, designed by R. A. Hill and W. L. Vernon, contained 1400 seats and had a 'grand organ' formerly used in Lichfield Cathedral. Under the direction of Dr. John Abram concerts featuring many famous artists took place in the building but during the first World War these were abandoned and later the hall was converted into the Elite Cinema and eventually burned down. The site has remained vacant for some 30 years.

153. (*right*) St. Mary Magdalen, just off Warrior Square, was designed in 1852 by Frederick Marrable, the tower with its beacon turret being added in 1872. The church is very typical of the town—showing a nice combination of a sloping corner site and local stone.

154. The east side of Warrior Square as it is today showing (left) a major infill erected in 1971 — a block of G.L.C. flats designed by Gotch & Partners. On the extreme right is the bronze statue of Queen Victoria, unveiled by the Marquess of Abergavenny, Lord Lieutenant of Sussex, on 31 December 1902. In the background is the Church of St. Mary Magdalen.

155. (*left*) Turning into London Road from Kings Road, St. Leonards presents the visitor with a fascinating array of 19th-century church architecture. On the left is the small remaining section of the first Christ Church (1860); then the impressive new Christ Church (1875), while behind is the Congregational Church, one of the finest non-conformist buildings in Sussex, founded in 1863 by James Griffin and designed by Habershon, Spalding & Brock.

156. (*below left*) Christ Church St. Leonards was designed by Sir Arthur Blomfield and opened in May 1875. The tower shown here, was added later in 1894. This church can claim to be Blomfield's finest achievement in Sussex and one of the main centres of Anglo Catholic worship in southern England.

157. (*below right*) St. John's Upper Maze Hill, showing the octagonal tower with remodelled spire, baptistry and west wall of the nave — the only portions remaining of the church designed by Blomfield in 1881. The rest of the church is a replacement by H. S. Goodhart-Rendel (1951) following extensive bomb damage in 1943. St. John's began as a temporary daughter church to Christ Church in 1867.

158.   A group of scholars and teachers at the Melrose College for Young Ladies, De Charm Road, St. Leonards, in about 1895. The College, described as a 'superior home school for the daughters of gentlemen', was run by the Misses Lee and Davis, and had a reputation for its 'efficiency and resources'.

159. (*left*) Father Charles Lyndhurst Vaughan, first Rector of St. Leonards was formerly Vicar of St. Neots, Huntingdonshire and came to St. Leonards in 1863. It was due to his efforts that Christ Church was built in 1875 and the tradition of Anglo Catholic worship begun in the parish.

160. (*right*) The novelist Sheila Kaye-Smith (1887-1956) from a photograph *c.*1920. She was born in St. Leonards and in 1924 married the Rev. T. Penrose Fry, a Curate of Christ Church, London Road. In 1919 Sheila Kaye-Smith published *Tamarisk Town* a novel set in Marlingate (*i.e.* Hastings) in which the chief character, Edward Monypenny, becomes Mayor and is obsessed with plans to make the town a really first class resort!

161. (*above*) The original design for St. Peter's Bohemia by James Brooks. The church was erected in 1885, in the subdivided parish of St. Paul, with £14,300 presented by Miss Blanche E. Elliott.

162. The attractive Gothic Park Road Methodist Church, Bohemia, was designed by Philip H. Tree and erected in 1891-2. Methodist worship was established in the Bohemia area in about 1876 by John Surman, and in 1880 the present site was acquired and a School-Chapel opened soon after.

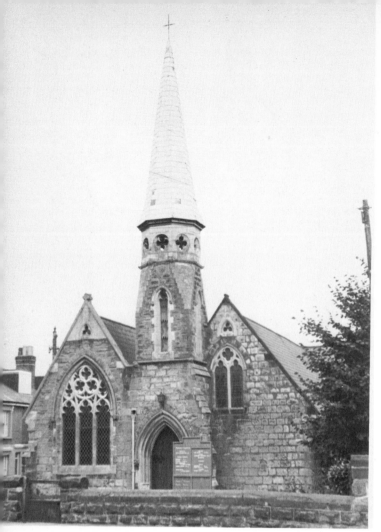

163. The Presbyterian Church (now U.R.C.) of St. Luke, Silverhill which claims to be one of the earliest Presbyterian foundations in the south of England, was established by Doctor William Boyd in 1854. The church has been enlarged over the years, the tower and spire being added in 1865, and the chancel and hall in 1909.

164. Members of the Salvation Army collecting 'Jam jars, rags, bones etc.' in aid of the Self Denial Fund at Silverhill in 1910.

165. A fine assembly of trams about to start for the annual outing of the Mount Pleasant Congregational Church in 1908. An electric tramway was opened in Hastings during the late summer of 1905, and eventually the system had a track length of nearly 20 miles. To avoid unsightly overhead wires the Dolter surface contact 'stud' method was employed for some time along the seafront line.

166. (*left*) St. Leonard's Hollington, known as the 'Church in the Wood' was extensively restored in 1865-6, when the present chancel was erected. Charles Lamb was much taken by the (then) isolated situation of the building, remarking that it stood 'like the first idea of a church, before parishioners were thought of'.

167. Castleham, a mansion situated on a commanding site some distance north of Hollington Church, was built by David Henry Stone in about 1868. A delightful example of mid-Victorian Gothic, the house was demolished in 1977. The area is now an industrial estate.

168. (*left*) The fine Silverhill smock mill, also known as Draper's Mill, after its owners from 1849 until 1961. The mill ceased working in 1941, but after years of neglect, suffered severe storm damage in 1961 and was demolished. A mill existed on the site in 1813, and in 1838, this was replaced by one brought from West Hill by a miller named Harmer. Later it was reconstructed (1862), but burned down in 1865, and rebuilt as seen here by John Upfield of Catsfield in 1866.

169. (*below*) The former Baldslow Mill now a private house. This smock mill, sometimes called Harrow Mill, was built by Upfields of Catsfield in 1857, and following the loss of its sails in 1900 continued to grind by steam power until *c*.1930, when it was purchased by a Mr. F. Richmond who converted it in 1933.

170. (*left*) Augustus John Cuthbert Hare, biographer and travel writer came from an East Sussex family and was born in Rome in 1834. He lived on the continent for many years but returned to England in 1870 and died at Holmhurst, Baldslow in 1903. Hare chose only the best people as friends — the King of Sweden among them — and is remembered for his lengthy autobiography *The Story of My Life* (1896-1900).

171. The old church of St. Helen's, Ore, which was replaced by the present church in 1869. In 1868 it was stated that 'the whole interior is so damp and wretched that parishioners are prevented from attending'. Consequently a faculty was obtained to build a new church on a nearby site utilizing suitable material from the old one. A ruined portion of the old St. Helen's still survives.

172. (*above*) A photograph of St. Helen's Ore dating from about 1905 showing the original spire which was a much admired landmark in the district when the new church was erected in 1869. The spire was taken down in 1966.

173. An engraving dated 20 November 1849, of St. Clement's Chapel and Parsonage at Halton. The Church was designed by Thomas Catley in 1838, and the cost of erection was born by the Countess Waldegrave. St. Clements was closed in 1970 and later demolished.

174. A late 19th-century picture of one of the area's great tourist attractions — Fairlight Glen, which could be visited by waggonette daily from Hastings. Visitors were urged 'not to miss this exquisite piece of scenery', which included the 'cool, sequested and romantic Dripping Well'.

175. (*above*) The famous Lovers' Seat, Fair access to all but the hale and sturdy — much story of the seat, concerning a young lady fr long to tell here . . . .

176. (*below*) Fairlight windmill in about 18 and in 1819 it was rebuilt as a smock mill by eventually burned down in 1869. In the dist

...e described as 'A place — though somewhat difficult of
...with visitors'. This statement still holds good — but the
...hurst and an officer commanding a revenue cutter, is too

...was recorded on this site in 1462 worked by a John Watts,
...as Webster. Later it was leased to William Crisford, and
...e seen the 'Priory mills' clustered on West Hill.

177. (below) Victorian promotion of the romantic
charms of Fairlight Glen included this advertisement
of what must have been a very special scent costing 5p
per bottle!

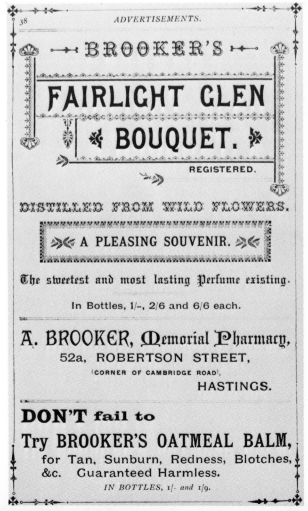

178. St. Andrew's Church, Fairlight, in about 1905. The church replaced a much older building in 1845, and was designed by T. Little. The interior contains a monument (1881) to W. and E. J. Jansen by J. S. Westmacott.

179. Beauport on the outskirts of Hastings (now an hotel) was the residence of General James Murray from about 1766 till his death in 1795. The General married Cordelia, a daughter of John Collier in 1748, and later became Governor of Quebec in 1759. 'Beauport' was the name of a village near Quebec where Murray distinguished himself in action against the French. The photograph dates from around 1900 and shows the house as largely rebuilt in c.1860.

SELECT BIBLIOGRAPHY

BAINES, J. Manwaring, *Burton's St. Leonards*, Hastings, Hastings Museum, 1956. 68pp., illus.

BAINES, J. Manwaring, *Historic Hastings*, 2nd ed. Hastings, F. J. Parsons, Ltd., 1963. 437pp., illus., bibliog. First published 1955.

BAINES, J. Manwaring, and others, *The History of Hastings Grammar School, 1619-1966*, revised ed. Hastings, Governors of Hastings Grammar School Foundation, 1967. 324pp., illus. First published 1956.

BALL, F. C., *One of the damned: the life and times of Robert Tressell, author of the Ragged Trousered Philanthropist*. Weidenfeld and Nicolson, 1973. 266pp., illus.

BALL, F. C., *Tressell of Mugsborough*. Lawrence and Wishart, 1951. 224pp., illus.

BANNISTER, H. O., and TURNER, J., eds., *Picturesque Hastings*. Souvenir of the conference of the National Union of Teachers, Easter, 1908. Henry Frowde, O.U.P., Hodder & Stoughton [1908]. 255pp., illus.

BELT, Anthony, ed., *Hastings: a survey of times past and present, by members of the Hastings Natural History Society and others*. Hastings, Kenneth Saville, 1937. 259pp.

BRASSEY, Mrs. Anna, *A Voyage in the 'Sunbeam': our home on the ocean for eleven months. . .* Longmans, Green & Co., 1878. 511pp., illus., maps.

BRODRIBB, Gerald, *Hastings and men of letters*, 2nd ed. Old Hastings Preservation Society, 1971. 51pp., illus. First published 1953. Contains a list of novels set in Hastings.

BULLOCK, F. W. B., *The History of the parish church of St. Helen, Ore Sussex*. St. Leonards-on-Sea, Budd & Gillatt, 1951. 115pp.

BULLOCK, F. W. B., *A History of the 'Church-in-the-Wood', Hollington, Sussex*. St. Leonards-on-Sea, Budd & Gillatt, 1949, 302pp.

COLE, Thomas H., *The Antiquities of Hastings and the battlefield. . .* new ed. Hastings, Hastings and St. Leonards Philosophical Society, 1884. 238pp., maps, plans. First published 1867.

COLEMAN, George D., 'Hastings and St. Leonards waterworks, 1830-1970'. Hastings, County Borough of Hastings Water Committee, 1971. 126pp. Duplicated typescript.

COOPER, William Durrant, and ROSS, Thomas, 'Notices of Hastings and its municipal rights', *Sussex Archaeological Collections*, vol. 14 (1862), pp. 65-118, illus.

COUSINS, Henry, *Hastings of bygone days—and the present. . .* Hastings, F. J. Parsons, Observer Office, 1911. 304pp., illus.

CRAKE, W. V., 'The Correspondence of John Collier . . . and his connection with the Pelham family'. *Sussex Archaeological Collections*, vol. 45 (1902), pp. 62-109, illus.

DAWSON, Charles, *History of Hastings Castle, the castlery, rape and Battle of Hastings, to which is added a history of the collegiate church within the castle and its prebends*. 2 vols. Constable, 1909.

DAWSON, Charles, 'Note on the Hastings Corporation relics of coronations of the Kings and Queens of England', *Sussex Archaeological Collections*, vol. 45 (1902), pp. 110-113.

DIPLOCK, William, *The Hand-book for Hastings, St. Leonard's. . .* Hastings, Wm. Diplock; London, Simpkin Marshall & Co., 1845. 228pp., illus., folding map.

DYER, W. H. and VINT, A. K., *'Winkle Up!' The Story of the Hastings Winkle Club*. Hastings, The Winkle Club, 1972. 72pp., illus.

DYMOND, T. S., *The Memoirs of a Mayor of Hastings, 1926-7*. Hastings, F. J. Parsons, 1928. 148pp., illus.

FITTON, William H., *A Geological sketch of the vicinity of Hastings*. H. G. Wood, 1833. 94pp., illus.

FOWKE, Frank Rede, *The Bayeux Tapestry: a history and description*, G. Bell, 1913, 139pp., illus.

FUNNELL, Barny, *Christ Church, St. Leonards-on-Sea, 1859-1975*. St. Leonards-on-Sea, Budd & Gillatt [1975] 65pp., illus.

HARPER, Charles G., *The Hastings Road and the 'Happy Springs of Tunbridge'*. Illustrated by the Author. Chapman & Hall, 1906. 287pp.

HARRISON, James M., *[George] Bristow and the Hastings [bird] rarities affair*. [St. Leonards-on-Sea, A. H. Butler, 1968] 160pp., illus., facsims.

Hastings and St. Leonards in the Front Line: the story of the Borough's Bombing Ordeal. *Hastings and St. Leonards Observer*, Hastings, c.1946. 64pp., illus.

LEMMON, Charles H., *The Field of Hastings*. St. Leonards-on-Sea, Budd & Gillatt, 1957. 68pp., illus., plan.

MACKNESS, James, *Hastings considered as a resort for invalids. . .* John Constable, 1842. 151pp., tables.

MARSDEN, Peter, *The wreck of the Amsterdam*. Hutchinson, 1974. 288pp., illus.

MARSHALL, M. A. N., *Hastings Saga* [the seafaring family of Wenham]. Saint Catherine Press Ltd., 1953. 52pp., illus.

MARTIN, David, 'Hastings Augustinian Priory: an excavation report', *Hastings Area Archaeological Papers No. 2*. Hastings Archaeological Group, 1973. 46pp., illus., diagrs.

MONTGOMERY, Elizabeth, *The Story of Silverhill and St. Lukes: Our heritage*. St. Leonards [1978]. 92pp., illus.

MOSS, W. G., *The History and antiquities of the town and port of Hastings, illustrated by a series of engravings, from original drawings by W. G. Moss, draughtsman to His Royal Highness the Duke of Cambridge*. Kennington, W. G. Moss, 1824. 207pp., illus., map.

MURRAY, K. M. E., *Constitutional history of the Cinque Ports*. Manchester University Press, 1935. 282pp., bibliog.

NICOLL, Henrietta C., *The Story of Christ Church, St. Leonards-on-Sea*. Ed. by A. Clifton Kelway. St. Leonards-on-Sea, C. Whittaker, 1909. 80pp., illus., Quarto.

PAGE, William, and others, 'The Rape and Honour of Hastings: the Borough of Hastings with St. Leonards'. *Victoria County History of Sussex*, vol. 9 (1937), pp. 1-33, illus.

ROSS, Thomas, 'Hastings Documents', *Sussex Archaeological Collections*, vol. 23 (1871), pp. 85-118.

RUDLING, David R., 'Excavations in Winding Street, Hastings, 1975', *Sussex Archaeological Collections*, vol. 114 (1976), pp. 164-175, illus.

SALZMAN, L. F., *Hastings*, S.P.C.K., 1921. 126pp., illus., bibliog. (The Story of the English Towns.)

SAYER, C. L. ed., *Correspondence of Mr. John Collier . . . and his family, 1716-1780*. 2 vols. G. F. Hodgson & Son, 1907.

[STELL, John] *The Hasting's Guide; or, a description of that Ancient Town and Port and its Environs . . . By an Inhabitant*. London, Printed for J. Stell at his Circulating Library, Hastings; and by T. N. Longman, Pater-noster-Row . . . 1794. 124pp., illus., map.

STENTON, Sir John, and others, *The Bayeux Tapestry: a comprehensive survey*, 2nd ed. Phaidon, 1965. 194pp., illus., (some col.) bibliog., Quarto.

TEILHARD DE CHARDIN, Pierre, *Letters from Hastings 1908-1912. Introduction by Henri de Lubac*, S.J., New York, Herder & Herder, 1968. 206pp. First published by Aubier, Paris, 1965. Teilhard de Chardin was trained at the Jesuit Seminary at Ore Place.

SOME DATES IN THE HISTORY OF HASTINGS

771	Offa, King of Mercia subjugated the Hastingi.
928	Mint established at Hastings.
1066	The Battle of Hastings.
1094	William Rufus stormbound at Hastings on his way to France.
1265	Four Barons of Hastings summoned to Simon de Montfort's Parliament.
1287	Great storm devastated the harbour.
1339	Fishing fleet destroyed by French raiders.
1356	The Hastings Custumal compiled.
1377	Hastings sacked by the French.
1412	Grant of Hastings Rape to Sir John Pelham.
1436	The town again attacked by the French.
1589	Charter of Incorporation: Thomas Hay became first Mayor.
1595	Harbour rebuilt.
1643	Town guns surrendered to the Parliamentarian Colonel Morley.
1660	The Anabaptist Samuel Oates became Rector of All Saints'.
1700	New Town Hall built.
1707	John Collier became Town Clerk.
1739	Affray with smugglers at Bulverhythe.
1748	The *Amsterdam* wrecked at Bulverhythe.
1749	First fire engine presented to the town by James Pelham, M.P., and Andrew Stone, M.P.
1759-60	Board of Ordnance acquired land and constructed the Battery.
1766	East Fort rebuilt.
1768	The notorious smuggling gang known as 'Ruxey's Crew' broken up and 13 men executed.
1778	Military camp established at Ore.
1791	Barry's Circulating Library opened in East Parade.
1792	Tilden, Shadwell and others established the Town's first Bank (later Hastings Old Bank) at 90, High Street.
1794	First Hastings Guide published by John Stell.
1801	Sir Thomas Pelham created 1st Earl of Chichester
1804	Halton Barracks opened.
1806	Sir Arthur Wellesley (later Duke of Wellington) arrived in Hastings.
1806	Marine Parade begun.
1810	The artist J. M. W. Turner active in Hastings.
1813	Application for the erection of a theatre rejected by the Magistrates.
1818	The Society of Antiquaries sent William Stothard to Bayeux to make a complete copy of the Bayeux Tapestry.
1820	Hastings Paving and Improvement Act passed.
1823	Charles Lamb stayed in Hastings.
1823	Hare and Hounds Theatre, Ore, closed down.
1824	Pelham Crescent begun.
1824	Excavations carried out at Hastings Castle by William Herbert.
1825	New Theatre in Bourne Street opened
1828	New town of St. Leonards begun.
1830	*The Hastings Iris*, the town's first newspaper, began weekly publication.

1830	First gas lighting installed from a works established on site of Old Priory Mill.
1831	Hastings Literary and Scientific Society formed.
1832	St. Leonards Improvement Act passed.
1833	Public water supply begun.
1833	Mechanics Institute opened.
1833	Prince George of Cumberland laid foundation stone of a new market in George Street.
1834	Duchess of Kent with her daughter Princess (later Queen) Victoria stayed at 57 Marina (now Crown House).
1834-5	The White Rock headland removed.
1836	Police force established.
1840	Hastings and St. Leonards Cricket Club founded.
1842	The first Hastings Lifeboat, *Ariel* built by James Tutt.
1842	The Old Hospital opened in High Street.
1854	New Post Office opened at 2, Wellington Place.
1858	First official Lifeboat, the *Victoria*, launched.
1858	Hastings and St. Leonards Philosophical Society founded.
1860	Dante Gabriel Rossetti and Elizabeth Siddall married at St. Clement's church.
1861	Town Fire Brigade formed by William Glenister and James Tutt.
1862	Albert Memorial erected.
1862	Hastings Chess Club formed.
1863	Queens Hotel opened.
1864	Priory Cricket and Recreation Ground opened.
1870	Rotunda fish market opened.
1872	Hastings Pier opened.
1874	Public Baths on White Rock Parade opened by Thomas Brassey.
1877	*Hastings and St. Leonards Observer* office opened in Clermont (moved to Cambridge Road 1925).
1878	Hastings Grammar School founded by amalgamation of the Parker and Saunders endowments plus a grant from the Magdalen Charity.
1879	Royal Concert Hall opened in Warrior Gardens.
1882	Hastings and St. Leonards Electric Light Co. set up.
1887	Hastings Cricket Festival founded by Captain Greatrex and William Carless.
1888	Conservatoire founded by the local organist Dr. John Abram.
1890	Hastings Harbour Act passed.
1891	Lord and Lady Brassey open St. Leonards Pier.
1893	Company formed to construct harbour.
1895	The St. Leonards Archway demolished.
1895	First Hastings Chess Tournament held.
1897	Borough extended to include Ore and part of Hollington.
1899	The Winkle Club founded.
1903	Augustus Hare died at Holmbush, Baldslow.
1905	Electric trams introduced.
1914	Publication of Robert Tressell's novel *The Ragged Trousered Philanthropists*.
1919	Municipal Orchestra formed under Julian Clifford.
1919	Publication of Sheila Kaye-Smith's novel *Tamerisk Town*.
1923	Royal East Sussex Hospital opened in Bohemia Road.
1924	John Logie Baird (1888-1946) carried out successful experiments in television at 8, Queen's Arcade.
1927	Hastings bcomes last borough to adopt the Public Libraries Acts.
1927	White Rock Pavilion opened by the Duke of Windsor, Prince of Wales.
1928	New Museum opened at John's Place.
1928	Trolleybus service replaces trams.
1929	South Colonnade demolished.
1931	Rebuilt Hastings railway Station opened.
1943	March 11. Worst air raid of the war killed 38 people.
1944	May 12. Town visited by Mr. Winston Churchill, Field-Marshall Smuts and Mackenzie King.

1946	Winston Churchill installed as Lord Warden of the Cinque Ports.
1951	Princess Elizabeth visited Hastings.
1952	Old Hastings Preservation Society formed by the Reverend J. R. Sankey.
1956	Fishermen's Museum opened.
1957	Sir Winston Churchill received freedom of Hastings.
1961	Several Net Shops destroyed by fire.
1961	Silverhill windmill demolished.
1962	Publication of the *Hastings Town Development Plan*.
1964	St. Paul's Church demolished.
1966	Hastings celebrates the 900th anniversary of the Battle. The Royal School of Needlework commissioned to produce the Hastings Embroidery depicting 900 years of England's history in 27 panels.
1967	The Burton's St. Leonards Society formed.
1971	New Fire Station opened in Bohemia Road.
1971	Hastings Country Park (1500 acres) opened.
1971	Confirmation of the *Hastings Town Development Plan* in a slightly modified form.
1975	Commemorative plaque erected to the Hastings born author 'Grey Owl' (Archie Belaney, 1888-1938) in Hastings Country Park.
1978	Queen Elizabeth the Queen Mother opened the extension to the Stables Theatre.
1978	Stage production of *The Ragged Trousered Philanthropists* adapted by Stephen Lowe at the Riverside Studios, London.